STICKER DRESSING
PIRATES &
LONG AGO

PIRATES

Illustrated by Diego Diaz

Written by Kate Davies and Louie Stowell. Designed by Emily Bornoff
Historical consultant: Tony Pawlyn, National Maritime Museum Cornwall

Contents

When you see this sign ✳ it means the person it's
next to is a real pirate or another real character from history.

VIKING PIRATES

About a thousand years ago, seafarers from Norway, Sweden and Denmark - known as Vikings – terrorized the coasts of northern Europe. Vikings raided coastal towns and villages, stealing food and anything else that caught their eye. These Vikings are attacking a village in Ireland.

Thorfinn

Leif

Erik

3

THE QUEEN'S PIRATES

It's a little over 400 years ago, and John Hawkins and Francis Drake have just returned from long sea voyages. They're privateers – pirates who steal from foreign ships on the Queen's orders. Queen Elizabeth is thrilled, because they've brought her lots of Spanish gold.

Queen Elizabeth I ✷

John Hawkins ✳   Francis Drake ✳   5

BUCCANEERS

It's about 300 years ago, and pirates known as buccaneers are roaming the islands of the Caribbean Sea, off the coasts of Mexico and Central America. This buccaneer captain wears a magnificent silk coat, stolen from the captain of a merchant ship. He's giving orders to his scruffy new recruits. They hope to be successful pirates with ships of their own one day.

Buccaneer captain

Frank (new pirate)

Tom (cabin boy)

BELOW DECK

These pirates are busy below deck. The cook lost his leg in a skirmish and has a wooden one instead. So, he's more use in the kitchen than in a fight. The crew is lucky to have a surgeon on board. On some ships, the carpenter has to do the operations.

Cook

Joseph

MAROONED!

This pirate has been left all alone on a desert island, as a punishment for stealing from his fellow pirates. This is called marooning. He's been wearing the same tattered old clothes for months.

Marooned pirate

A RETIRED PIRATE

This wealthy gentleman was a pirate for most of his life. But now he's retired to spend his stolen fortune. He lives a relaxing life in a mansion on a Caribbean island – although he still trades with pirates to make even more money, when he feels like it.

Retired pirate

PIRATE PARTY

These pirates are having a party on board their ship. Their captain is known as 'Calico Jack' because he likes to wear striped breeches made from a fabric called calico.

Unusually for a pirate, Jack has women in his crew, including a famous pirate named Anne Bonny. Anne dresses up as a man, because women aren't allowed to be pirates.

Calico Jack ✳

First Mate
(second in command)

Anne Bonny ✳

15

PIRATE PORT

On an island in the Caribbean Sea is a pirate port known as Port Royal. It's where many pirates come to spend time off, repair their ships, or even to visit the doctor. The port is so full of pirates that they pretty well run the place. On shore, these pirates wear their finest clothes – stolen, of course.

William

Samuel

Nathaniel

BARBARY CORSAIRS

It's the 1720s, and the Golden Age of piracy is coming to an end. It's getting harder to be a pirate now. Countries such as Britain are building stronger navies, with well-armed ships that can usually beat pirate ships in battle. But, on the Barbary Coast, along the north coast of Africa, a band of fierce pirates known as corsairs has managed to sneak up on a British trading ship. The corsairs are about to take a passenger captive, to sell as a slave.

Sir John (a British passenger)

Selim

Kamal

19

CHINESE PIRATES

By the 1800s, piracy has almost died out in the Caribbean Sea and along the Barbary Coast. But off the coast of China it's a different story. Powerful Chinese pirates sail in boats known as junks, attacking ships carrying valuable cargoes such as silks and spices. This pirate captain is demanding payment from a local merchant. If he doesn't pay up, they'll attack.

Chinese pirate

Chinese pirate captain

Chinese merchant

THE PIRATES OF BORNEO

It's the 1830s, and the island of Borneo in the South China Sea is having some serious pirate trouble. An English sailor named James Brooke has agreed to help the local rulers crush these pirate pests – in return for being made "rajah" (ruler) of part of Borneo. He's attacking the pirates – known as Sea Dayaks – at their base on the shore.

Dayak with a blowpipe

Dayak spearman

James Brooke ✴

PIRATE FLAGS

Many pirates used a flag known as the Jolly Roger – showing a skull with crossed bones underneath – to warn ships to surrender. But some pirate captains had flags of their own. Use the stickers to make up your own personal pirate flags.

STICKER DRESSING
LONG AGO

Illustrated by Emi Ordás
Written by Megan Cullis
Designed by Lisa Verrall
History Consultant: Dr. Anne Millard

Contents

ANCIENT EGYPT

It's over 3,000 years ago, and a prince is visiting Egypt from a nearby land called Nubia. He has brought gifts, including gold and ostrich eggs, for the King of Egypt, the Pharaoh. The Pharaoh wears a red and white crown, and holds a pet leopard cub on a leash. Exotic animals are popular pets among wealthy Egyptians.

Prince of Nubia

Pharaoh

Guard

THE BYZANTINE EMPIRE

It's around 1,500 years ago, in a splendid palace in Constantinople – the capital of the Byzantine Empire, which stretched from Eastern Europe to the Middle East. Lots of important people have gathered to celebrate a religious feast. Everyone wears beautiful silk robes decorated with precious jewels.

Bishop

Emperor

Palace official

VIKINGS

Today is market day in a town in Scandinavia, about a thousand years ago. The people who live here are farmers, warriors, merchants and pirates – and we call them Vikings. The Viking merchant has just sailed back from Russia, bringing furs to sell in town. The warrior has returned with treasure from a raid overseas. He wears iron chain mail on his body.

Warrior

Farmer

Merchant

IN A MEDIEVAL CASTLE

It's 1406 and a castle is being built in Prussia – now part of Germany. The ruler of the German lands, known as the Holy Roman Emperor, has come to admire it. On his crown he wears a gold cross. He's greeted by a soldier called a Teutonic Knight. When it's finished, the castle will be the main headquarters of the Teutonic Knights. The chief stonemason is in charge of the building work.

Holy Roman Emperor

Teutonic Knight

Chief stonemason

THE GREAT WALL OF CHINA

On a winter's day in the 1400s, the Chinese Emperor is inspecting a huge wall which has recently been rebuilt to keep out enemy tribes. It's now known as the Great Wall of China. On his head, the Emperor wears a knotted cap to show his royal status. He's joined by his general in elaborate chain mail. A soldier, known as a standard bearer, carries the flag of his military unit.

Emperor

Standard bearer

General

THE AZTECS

It's 500 years ago on the streets of Tenochtitlan, the ancient capital city of the Aztec Empire. The Aztec people have come to watch their emperor on parade. He wears a crown made of brilliant green feathers and a bright woven cloak.

Aztec Emperor

SPANISH CONQUEROR

While the Aztecs are ruling in Mexico, a Spanish conqueror and his army are about to invade. They are planning to claim the land as their own, so this conqueror wears a metal suit in case he's attacked by the local people.

Spanish conqueror

THE MUGHAL EMPIRE

On a hot evening in 1653, the Emperor of the Mughal Empire in India is admiring his new monument, the Taj Mahal. The Emperor and the Prince, his son, wear light, airy robes to keep them cool. On their heads, they wear turbans decorated with rubies and emeralds. Even the guardsman's protective clothing is lightweight, so he doesn't get too hot.

Guardsman

Emperor

Prince

THE PALACE OF VERSAILLES

It's 1697 and the King of France is throwing a ball in his palace at Versailles. His young grandson, the Duke, has just been married, and lots of important nobles are attending the celebrations. The King's robe is embroidered with a flower design, known as the fleur-de-lis. All the men wear long, curly wigs, which are very fashionable.

Nobleman

Duke

King of France

AN ITALIAN COMEDY

It's 300 years ago and these actors are performing in an Italian comic play. The Captain is a cowardly soldier who carries a long sword. Pantalone is a greedy man who loves money. Harlequin uses a stick, called a slapstick, to hit people and make the audience laugh.

The Captain

Pantalone

Harlequin

EDO JAPAN

It's about 200 years ago on the streets of Edo – now called Tokyo. At this time, Edo was one of the largest cities in the world, and it was very wealthy. A fierce warrior, called a samurai, is on patrol. He's very important, and people show him great respect. The nobleman works for the government. He wears a silk robe, called a kimono. The actor wears face paint, ready to perform in a play.

Actor

Samurai

Nobleman

WILD WEST

It's about 150 years ago in the American West, and a cowboy is buying furs from a Native American chief. The sheriff of the local cowboy town is on his way to interview some workers who are looking for gold in the river. He hopes they can help him find the criminal he's chasing. The cowboy wears leather chaps to protect his legs when he's riding. The Native American chief wears a feather headdress, which was given to him by his tribe as a sign of great respect.

Native American chief

Cowboy

Sheriff

1920S GOLFER

On a fine day in the 1920s, an English gentleman is playing a round of golf. He wears fashionable golfing clothes – a patterned sweater and breeches called plus fours.

First published in 2012 by Usborne Publishing Ltd., 83-85 Saffron Hill, London, EC1N 8RT, England. www.usborne.com.

Golfer